Profiles of the Presidents

WILLIAM
McKINLEY

★ ★ ★

Profiles of the Presidents

WILLIAM McKINLEY

by Robin Doak

Content Adviser: Rich McElroy, Historian, McKinley Museum and National Memorial, Canton, Ohio

Reading Adviser: Dr. Linda D. Labbo, Department of Reading Education, College of Education, The University of Georgia

COMPASS POINT BOOKS ✦ MINNEAPOLIS, MINNESOTA

Compass Point Books
3109 West 50th Street, #115
Minneapolis, MN 55410

Visit Compass Point Books on the Internet at *www.compasspointbooks.com*
or e-mail your request to *custserv@compasspointbooks.com*

Photographs ©: Hulton/Archive by Getty Images, cover, 3, 12, 25, 28, 33, 38, 42, 43, 54 (bottom right),
55 (top right), 56 (bottom right), 57 (all), 58 (right), 59 (right); White House Collection, Courtesy White
House Historical Association (62), 6; Used by permission from The McKinley Museum, Canton, Ohio,
7, 10, 11 (top), 15, 16, 18, 26, 46, 48, 54 (left), 55 (left, all), 56 (left); Michael S. Yamashita/Corbis, 8;
Corbis, 9, 17, 20, 36; North Wind Picture Archives, 11 (bottom), 22, 37, 39, 50, 58 (bottom left),
59 (bottom left); Library of Congress, 13, 21, 23, 35, 41, 44, 45; Bettmann/Corbis, 14, 19, 31; Stock
Montage, 24, 47, 59 (top left); DVIC/NARA, 30, 32, 40, 58 (top left); Bruce Burkhardt/Corbis, 54
(top right); Union Pacific Museum Collection, 55 (bottom right); Denver Public Library, Western
History Collection, 56 (top right).

Editors: E. Russell Primm, Emily J. Dolbear, Melissa McDaniel, and Catherine Neitge
Photo Researcher: Svetlana Zhurkina
Photo Selector: Linda S. Koutris
Designer: The Design Lab
Cartographer: XNR Productions, Inc.

Library of Congress Cataloging-in-Publication Data
Doak, Robin S. (Robin Santos), 1963–
   William McKinley / by Robin Doak.
      p. cm. — (Profiles of the presidents)
   Summary: A biography of the twenty-fifth president of the United States, discussing his personal life,
education, and political career.
   Includes bibliographical references and index.
   ISBN 0-7565-0271-3 (hardcover : alk. paper)
   1. McKinley, William, 1843–1901—Juvenile literature. 2. Presidents—United States—Biography—
Juvenile literature. [1. McKinley, William, 1843–1901. 2. Presidents.] I. Title. II. Series.
   E711.6 .D63 2004
   973.8'8'092—dc21   2002153529

Table of Contents

★ ★ ★

*NOTE: In this book, words that are defined in the glossary are
in* **bold** *the first time they appear in the text.*

The End of an Era

★ ★ ★

Americans looked forward to a bright future as the United States entered the twentieth century. President William McKinley had led the nation to victory in a war against

William McKinley was the twenty-fifth U.S. president.

Spain. The economy was strong and healthy. In 1900, the popular president was reelected. However, just six months into his new term, McKinley was shot and killed in Buffalo, New York.

McKinley's **assassination** in September 1901 marked the end of an era. McKinley was the last president to serve during the nineteenth century. He was also the last Civil War (1861–1865) veteran elected to the White House.

◄ *McKinley as a soldier in the Civil War*

McKinley had been a highly respected president. After his death, however, some people did not think so highly of him. Historians painted him as a **puppet** of powerful advisers and big business. They remembered him as a weak president who was pushed into war by Congress and public opinion. In recent years, historians have taken a second look at McKinley. Now, many of them believe he was a strong leader.

Some historians think of McKinley as the first modern president. Under McKinley, the United States took control of a number of Pacific islands. This new "American **Empire**" included the Philippines, Guam, and Hawaii. McKinley also carefully managed foreign trade. He made sure that the United States would have the same chance to trade in China as other nations. President McKinley did much to help the United States become a world power.

A beach in Guam, a country that became part of President McKinley's new "American Empire"

Young William

★ ★ ★

William McKinley was born on January 29, 1843, in Niles, Ohio. He was the seventh of nine children born to William McKinley Sr., an iron manufacturer, and Nancy Campbell Allison McKinley. William McKinley Sr. had to work hard to support his large family.

Growing up in the tiny town of Niles, all of the McKinley children helped out at home. Like his brothers, William chopped wood, took care of the family cows, and worked in the yard. A smart, observant boy, William did well in Niles's one-room schoolhouse. Later, he would show

▾ William McKinley Sr. was an iron manufacturer whose work often took him far from home.

McKinley was born ▸
in this house
in Niles, Ohio.

talent in public speaking and debating. These skills
would serve him well as a politician.

When William was ten, the McKinleys moved to
Poland, Ohio, so that the children could attend Poland
Academy, a public school run by Methodists. The
Methodist religion was an important part of the McKinley household. As a teenager, William decided to become a minister. Although he later changed his mind,
he always remained a devout Christian. He attended
church on Sundays, and he often prayed before making
important decisions.

In 1860, seventeen-year-old William entered Allegheny College in Meadville, Pennsylvania. After just one term, though, he became ill and had to leave school. William intended to return to the college. By the time he regained his health, however, his family could no longer afford to pay for his schooling. Instead, William taught school and worked as a clerk in Poland's post office.

William was keenly interested in the social issues of the day. The most important issue was slavery. The Southern states allowed slavery. The Northern states banned it. Ohio, where William lived, did

▲ William McKinley as a young man

◀ Steamboats along the Ohio River, which was the dividing line between states that allowed slavery and those that did not

not allow slavery. Directly south of Ohio lay Kentucky, where slavery was allowed. The Ohio River separated the two states. It was the last challenge runaway slaves faced when fleeing to freedom in the North.

William listened carefully to discussions and arguments about slavery. Like the rest of the McKinley family, he was strongly against slavery. In 1861, the issue finally split the nation in two. By May, eleven Southern states seceded, or withdrew, from the Union and formed the Confederate States of America. President Abraham Lincoln did not think the Southern states had any right to leave the Union. Lincoln would do whatever he could to stop them.

Slaves planting ▶ sweet potatoes on a South Carolina plantation in 1862

A Natural Politician

★ ★ ★

In April 1861, the Civil War broke out between Northern and Southern states. It would prove to be the bloodiest war in the history of the United States. McKinley was a strong supporter of the Northern cause. After discussing it with his mother, McKinley signed up to fight for the Union army.

▾ The Battle of Shiloh took place in Hardin County, Tennessee, in April 1862. It was one of the bloodiest battles of the Civil War.

Rutherford B. Hayes was a colonel in the Civil War and became president in 1877.

McKinley served under Colonel Rutherford B. Hayes, an Ohioan who would one day become the nineteenth U.S. president. The young McKinley fought in a number of bloody battles. He impressed other soldiers with his bravery, and he rose in rank as the years passed. Hayes was one of McKinley's biggest supporters. He called McKinley "one of the bravest and finest officers in the army." By the end of the war, McKinley had gained the rank of brevet major. For the rest of his life, people would call him "the Major."

After the war, McKinley went to Albany, New York, to study law. In 1867, he passed the exam that allowed him to practice law in Ohio. McKinley set up an office in Canton, Ohio. He was handsome, good-natured, and

had high ideals. Many
people thought he had a
bright future.

In 1867, Rutherford
B. Hayes ran as the Re-
publican **candidate** for
governor of Ohio. Mc-
Kinley, also a Republican,
helped out during the
campaign. With his hard
work and excellent speak-
ing skills, it soon became
clear that McKinley was a
natural politician.

▲ *McKinley's law office in Canton, Ohio*

Republican party offi-
cials took notice of the young man. A year later, they
chose him to run as prosecuting attorney of Stark County in Ohio. The prosecuting attorney was in charge of
making the case against people accused of committing
crimes in the county. McKinley won the election, even
though the people of Stark County usually voted for
Democrats. It was McKinley's first time to be elected
to public office.

In 1869, McKinley began courting Ida Saxton, the frail, beautiful daughter of a wealthy banker. On January 25, 1871, the two married. Later that year, their daughter Katherine was born. Life seemed promising for the young family. Over the next few years, however, a series of events deeply affected Ida McKinley. In 1873, her mother died. Shortly after that, Ida gave birth to a second daughter, also named Ida, who died within five months. Then, in 1875, three-year-old Katherine died of typhoid fever.

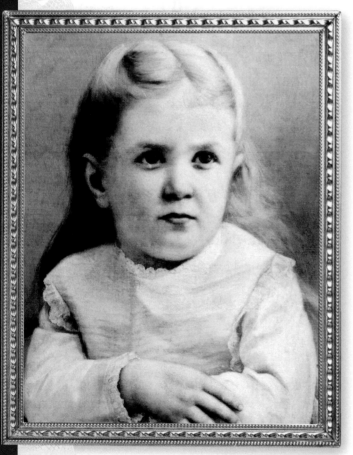

Katherine McKinley died in 1875 at the age of three.

This string of disasters shattered Ida, both mentally and physically. She became ill and later developed epilepsy, a condition that causes **seizures.** For the rest of her life, Ida was a fragile, sickly woman. She spent much of her time in bed or in a rocking chair. Still, she

★

kept busy. Over the years Ida knitted more than seven thousand pairs of slippers, which she gave to needy children, war veterans, and friends. McKinley gave his wife much love and attention and did his best to care for her.

With the loss of his two daughters and a sick and unhappy wife at home, McKinley threw himself into politics. In 1876, he was elected to the U.S. House of Representatives. He and Ida moved into a hotel in Washington, D.C. In the nation's capital, the Ohioan's warm, easygoing personality earned him many friends and admirers.

▲ *Ida McKinley in the late 1800s; she was deeply affected by the death of her mother and two daughters.*

As a congressman, McKinley spoke out on many issues. He favored giving African-Americans the right to vote. McKinley also wanted to change the way people who worked for the government were hired and promoted to make it more fair. In addition, he spoke out against some of the actions of big businesses. McKinley's main interest, however, was tariffs. A tariff is a tax on goods brought into the country. McKinley believed that taxing foreign goods coming into the United States was the best way to protect and strengthen American industries. He thought that by making foreign goods more costly, people would be more likely to buy products made in America.

McKinley was ▼ an outspoken congressman.

McKinley's proudest moment in Congress came with the passage of the McKinley Tariff Act in 1890. The act, which McKinley wrote, placed high taxes on certain goods from other countries. This act also gave the president the power to raise or lower tariffs as he saw fit.

Not everyone liked the McKinley Tariff Act. Many Americans were angered at the new, higher prices placed on foreign goods. Others believed that the tariff only helped the large American companies producing goods that competed with foreign products. For this reason, some people began calling McKinley "the friend of big business." Partly as a result of the tariff act, McKinley was not reelected in November 1890.

◄ An 1890 political cartoon has McKinley boxing for his tariff act.

McKinley and the Kingmaker

★ ★ ★

McKinley was not out of politics for long. In 1891, he ran for governor of Ohio and won. As governor, McKinley made changes to the tax laws of Ohio. He also improved

Coal miners on strike ▶ in Washingtonville, Ohio, in 1894

President William McKinley (second from left in the front) and First Lady Ida McKinley visit Mount Holyoke College in South Hadley, Massachusetts, in 1899. Despite her seizures, Ida insisted on performing many official duties of a first lady.

working conditions for laborers and quickly ended an 1894 coal miners' **strike** that had turned violent.

Being governor did not place heavy demands on Mc-Kinley's schedule. He still could spend plenty of time with Ida. Despite her illness, Ida insisted on remaining by her husband's side whenever possible. At official parties or dinners, McKinley would watch his wife carefully for any signs that she might have a seizure. If he saw one coming on, he would lead her from the room or place a napkin over her face until it passed. This happened many times while he was governor and continued after he was elected president. Even then, Ida refused to give up several of her duties as

Mark Hanna was one of McKinley's most important friends and advisers.

White House hostess. She insisted on attending social events. This was a brave attitude at a time when many ill people were kept hidden from the world.

In 1893, McKinley's political career was nearly ruined. That year, he signed some bank papers for a friend who had fallen on hard times. When his friend went broke, McKinley discovered he was required to repay his friend's debt of $130,000.

Several friends of McKinley's quickly stepped in to help. One of them was a wealthy Ohio businessman named Mark A. Hanna. He admired McKinley and agreed with his views on the important issues of the day. Throughout McKinley's political career, Hanna supported and encouraged his friend. Over the years, he would act as McKinley's campaign manager, fund-raiser, and adviser.

Hanna donated some of his own money to pay back McKinley's debts. He encouraged his wealthy friends to chip in, too. Many others stepped forward to aid McKinley, including Civil War **veterans,** miners, farmers, and Ohioans who admired the governor. McKinley escaped ruin, and he was reelected governor in 1893.

By that time, both McKinley and Hanna had a bigger political prize in mind: the U.S. presidency. In 1895, Hanna began preparing for the 1896 presidential election. As McKinley's campaign manager, Hanna worked hard to see that McKinley would become the Republican candidate for president. He lined up supporters and ran an expensive campaign to impress Republican Party leaders. Hanna's efforts paid off, and McKinley was chosen. Republicans then picked Garret A.

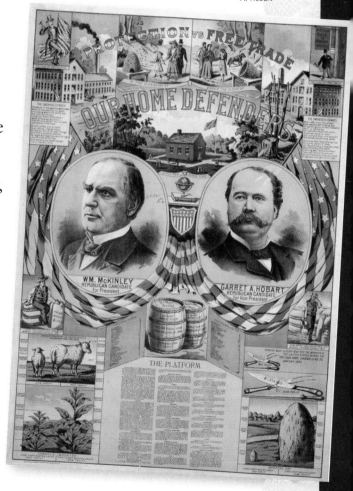

▼ *A Republican campaign poster from 1896 showing running mates William McKinley (left) and Garret A. Hobart*

William Jennings Bryan was the Democratic candidate for president in 1896.

Hobart, a lawyer from New Jersey, as their vice presidential candidate.

The main issue of the campaign was the nation's monetary system. Some people wanted a gold standard. With a gold standard, anyone could bring their paper money to the government and exchange it for gold. Other Americans favored free silver, meaning that the government could make an unlimited supply of silver coins. This would increase the nation's money supply and lower the amount any individual dollar was worth. Some Americans preferred a system that combined the use of both silver and gold. McKinley followed his party's wishes and supported gold.

The Democrat running against McKinley was former Nebraska congressman William Jennings Bryan. He favored free silver. Bryan believed that a gold standard allowed a few wealthy people to control the nation. Free silver, on the other hand, helped people who were in debt because it made the money they owed worth less. Bryan traveled around the country, making fiery speeches in favor of silver to all who would listen. He had little campaign money to work with, but he traveled 18,000 miles (29,000 kilometers) in just three months.

▼ *William McKinley on the porch of his home in Canton, Ohio, during the 1896 election*

Thanks to Hanna's wealth and ability to raise money, McKinley had nearly $6 million to spend on his campaign. Hanna printed up millions of pamphlets, campaign buttons, and posters. He also used campaign funds to pay the train fare for people wanting to travel to Canton, Ohio, where McKinley lived. More than 750,000 people made the trip to McKinley's house to listen to him speak from his front porch.

McKinley talked in plain terms about the important issues of the day. He promised listeners

William McKinley being sworn in as the twenty-fifth president of the United States in March 1897; outgoing President Grover Cleveland is to the right.

"good work, good wages, and good money." His plainspoken yet dignified personality impressed people and won him many votes. After hearing him speak, one listener remarked, "He does not talk wildly, and his appearance is that of a president."

On Election Day in November, fifty-three-year-old William McKinley received just over half of all the votes cast. He would soon be sworn in as the nation's twenty-fifth president. His mother Nancy commented, "Oh God, keep him humble."

An American Empire

★ ★ ★

After taking the oath of office on March 4, 1897, McKinley quickly went to work. One of his first acts as president was to convince Congress to pass the Dingley Tariff Act. The new tariffs were the highest yet to be placed on

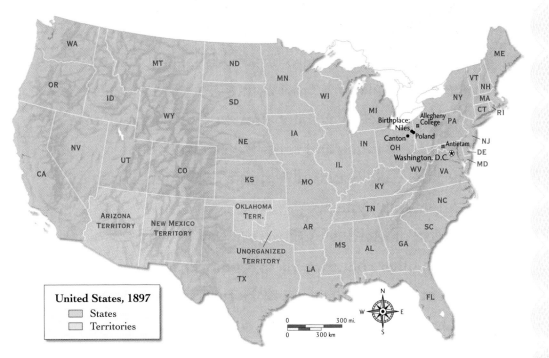

United States, 1897
- ☐ States
- ☐ Territories

Cuban rebels in 1896

foreign goods. The act also helped McKinley make new trade agreements with other countries.

During McKinley's first term, he worked to improve the system of hiring and firing federal workers. He also signed the Gold Standard Act, which kept the United States on a gold-only system.

Most of McKinley's first term, however, was spent dealing with other countries. At that time, Spain controlled the island of Cuba off the coast of Florida. The Cuban people resented Spanish rule. In 1895, some Cubans rebelled. To prevent the Spanish from making money, the rebels burned farms and ranches throughout the island. The Spaniards brutally put down the rebellion and imprisoned hundreds of thousands of Cubans in camps.

The United States had a financial interest in Cuba. Many Americans owned land and grew sugar on the island. By the time McKinley took office in 1897, Americans had lost about $16 million in Cuba because of the uprising.

At first, the president tried to persuade Spain to give Cuba its independence. McKinley did not want to become directly involved in any fighting against Spain. Though many Americans believed that military action should be taken, the president held strong. By January 1898, however, it was clear to McKinley that Spain would never leave Cuba without a fight. He decided to send the battleship USS *Maine* to Havana, Cuba, to show Spain that he was willing to protect American interests there.

Americans followed the Cuban crisis in the newspapers. Each day, papers printed exaggerated stories about dying Cubans, courageous Cuban freedom fighters, and the cruel Spaniards who kept them down. This type of reporting, known as yellow journalism, aroused strong public opinion against the Spanish.

The USS Maine entering the harbor of Havana, Cuba, in January 1898

On February 9, 1898, the *New York Journal* carried a letter written by Spain's **ambassador** to the United States. The letter had been captured on its way to Cuba. In the letter, the ambassador called McKinley "weak" and said that he was "a bidder for the admiration of the crowd." Americans were furious.

Less than a week later, on February 15, an explosion blew apart the USS *Maine* while it was in the harbor of Havana. More than two hundred and sixty men were killed. A naval court determined that a Spanish mine in the harbor had caused the disaster. Today, however, many people think the explosion might have come from deep within the ship itself.

Once again, Americans were outraged. Shortly after the disaster, newspapers began carrying the slogan, "Remember the *Maine* and to hell with Spain!" This became the rallying cry for Americans who wanted war with Spain.

▼ *The explosion of the USS* Maine *in February 1898*

On April 11, President McKinley asked Congress for a declaration of war against Spain "in the name of humanity, in the name of civilization, in behalf of endangered American interests which give us the right and the duty to speak

American soldiers ▸
board a transport to
fight in the Spanish-
American War.

◄ *Commodore
George Dewey*

and to act." Less than two weeks later, Congress agreed. The president could now use military force against the Spanish in Cuba.

The Spanish-American War was short, lasting just over three months. The first U.S. military action of the war took place on May 1, 1898, when Commodore George Dewey sailed into Manila Bay in the Philippines, a group of Pacific islands controlled by Spain. In the Philippines, Dewey became a national hero by destroying ten Spanish warships there. American troops later took control of the Philippines.

In late June, U.S. forces finally arrived in Cuba. On July 1, future president Theodore Roosevelt and his troop of soldiers, nicknamed the Rough Riders, defeated the Spanish in the Battle of San Juan Hill. Two days later, the U.S. Navy destroyed what was left of Spain's war fleet off the coast of Cuba. At about the same time, U.S. troops took control of Puerto Rico, another island in the Caribbean held by Spain. Realizing that they could not win the war, Spain began talks with the United States on how to end it.

In August, between the end of the war and the signing of the peace **treaty,** the United States took control of the Hawaiian Islands. Two years later, Hawaii would become a U.S. territory, making all Hawaiians U.S. citizens. At first, several congressmen were against adding the formerly independent kingdom to the United States. McKinley worked hard to change their minds.

Peace talks between the United States and Spain took place in November in Paris, France. During the peace talks, Spain finally gave the islands of Puerto Rico and Guam to the United States. Also, Spain agreed to hand over the Philippines to the U.S. government in

▼ *Colonel Theodore Roosevelt (center) and his Rough Riders after the battle of San Juan Hill*

McKinley (second from right) and other officials at the ratification of the Treaty of Paris in February 1899. Even though the treaty was signed in December 1898, it was not formally approved by Congress until two months later.

exchange for $20 million. The Treaty of Paris, signed on December 10, marked the end of Spain's overseas empire.

Many people were pleased with the new American empire. However, other Americans were unhappy with the peace treaty. These people believed that taking control of smaller, weaker nations went against everything the United States stood for.

America's new holdings came at a high price. In February 1899, people in the Philippines took up arms to drive out U.S. forces. Over the next three years, 60,000 American soldiers fought in the Philippines. More than 7,000 Americans were killed or wounded, and hundreds of thousands of Filipinos died.

During his presidency, McKinley had the good fortune to be surrounded by capable men he could rely upon. One such man was William Howard Taft. After the war in the Philippines, McKinley chose Taft to set up a government there. Years later, Taft would be elected the

▾ *A water buffalo drags guns into position for American forces in the Philippines in 1899.*

William Howard Taft ▶
helped McKinley
establish a government
in the Philippines after
the conflict there.

twenty-seventh president of the United States and would
serve as chief justice of the U.S. Supreme Court.

McKinley also relied heavily on John Hay. He served
as the **secretary of state** from 1898 to 1901. Hay worked
hard to establish an Open Door policy with China.

This policy made sure that the United States would have as equal an opportunity to trade with China as other nations did. There would be no tariffs that would help one nation over another. The Open Door policy set a standard for free trade and open markets around the world.

◄ *Secretary of State John Hay helped establish an Open Door policy with China.*

In the summer of 1900, McKinley sent more than two thousand troops to China to help put down the Boxer Rebellion. The Boxers were Chinese citizens who believed that their nation should be free from foreign and Christian influence. The rebellion began in 1899, when the Boxers started attacking and killing foreigners and Chinese Christians in their country. In June, the Boxers held a group of foreign ambassadors hostage. American troops and soldiers from other countries helped rescue the ambassadors and ended the rebellion.

A participant in ▼
the Boxer Rebellion
of 1900

A Nation Mourns

★ ★ ★

McKinley was a likable, honest leader. The president set aside an hour each day to meet with the public. During these visits, he gave away scarlet carnations, which were his favorite flowers. McKinley often traveled around the nation, talking with supporters about the events of the day and listening to public opinion. He enjoyed a good relationship with the press, although he did not give formal interviews and didn't allow reporters to quote him directly.

▼ *McKinley shared a good relationship with both the public and the press.*

Times were good for the United States during McKinley's presidency and this added to his popularity. The United States was one of the strongest powers in the world. At home, the nation enjoyed a healthy economy. McKinley called his term one of "**prosperity** at home and **prestige** abroad."

A Republican campaign poster from 1900 showing running mates William McKinley and Theodore Roosevelt

When McKinley announced that he would run for reelection in 1900, no one was surprised. Because Vice

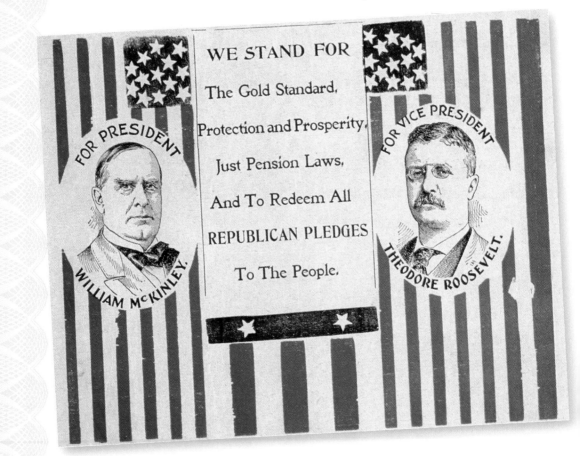

WE STAND FOR

The Gold Standard,

Protection and Prosperity,

Just Pension Laws,

And To Redeem All

REPUBLICAN PLEDGES

To The People.

FOR PRESIDENT

WILLIAM McKINLEY.

FOR VICE PRESIDENT

THEODORE ROOSEVELT.

President Garret Hobart had died while in office, Republicans had to look for another vice presidential candidate. They chose Theodore Roosevelt, the popular and energetic hero of the Spanish-American War.

The campaign in 1900 was much like the one in 1896. The Democratic Party again selected William Jennings Bryan as their candidate. Bryan again attacked the president on the gold standard. He also criticized McKinley for creating an American empire. As in 1896, Bryan traveled the country while McKinley remained at home. Just as he had in 1896, Mark Hanna managed McKinley's campaign. He spread McKinley's message of the nation's prosperity in pamphlets, postcards, and newspaper inserts.

▲ *William Jennings Bryan ran against McKinley again in 1900.*

When all the votes were counted, McKinley had defeated Bryan for yet a second time. As in the 1896 election, McKinley received over half of the votes cast.

McKinley being sworn into office in March 1901 ▾

In September 1901, McKinley traveled to Buffalo, New York, to attend the Pan-American Exposition. The exposition was a giant fair celebrating one hundred years of progress in North and South America. A number of new inventions were on display, including Thomas Edison's X-ray machine.

On September 5, McKinley spoke at the exposition. His speech before 50,000 people focused on the nation's bright future. He talked about the role of a powerful United States in the world. The following day, the president met the public inside the exposition's Temple of Music. Hundreds of people pushed toward McKinley, hoping to shake his hand. One man in the crowd was

▲ *A poster for the Pan-American Exposition in Buffalo, New York*

McKinley at the ▲ Pan-American exposition the day before he was shot

twenty-eight-year-old Leon Czolgosz, an unemployed mill worker. Czolgosz was also an anarchist, which is a person who rebels against all types of formal government and often uses violence.

As Czolgosz approached the president, he raised his hand and fired the gun he had been hiding. Czolgosz shot twice, hitting McKinley in the stomach and the chest. As Czolgosz was wrestled to the ground, McKinley's first thoughts were for his ailing wife, Ida. "My wife, be careful . . . how you tell her," McKinley said. "Oh be careful."

McKinley was taken to a small, dimly lit emergency hospital at the exposition. There, doctors worked to try to repair the damage done by the bullets. Although they

◀ *The shooting of President William McKinley on September 6, 1901*

Leon Czolgosz ▲ was convicted of murdering the president and was put to death in October 1901.

removed the bullet in the president's chest, they could not find the second bullet. Looking back, perhaps Edison's X-ray machine would have been helpful in locating it. Unfortunately, Edison was one of the few people who knew how to use the machine, and he was not there.

At first, McKinley's condition seemed to improve. The day after the shooting, doctors said that the president was doing well and that his injuries were not serious. However, he soon got worse. McKinley died on September 14. Vice President Theodore Roosevelt was sworn in as president that same day.

In prison, Czolgosz explained why he shot McKinley. He said, "I killed the president because he was the enemy of the people—the good working people." The

young man was later tried for the murder. He was convicted and put to death on October 29, 1901.

People across the nation mourned their slain president. His body was taken first to Buffalo City Hall
and then to Washington, D.C., where a funeral ceremony was held in the Capitol. Afterward, McKinley was
laid to rest in Canton, Ohio. On the day of his funeral,
Americans observed a five-minute period of silence. All

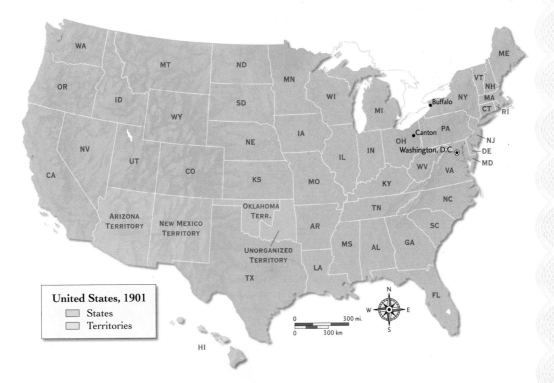

United States, 1901
States
Territories

McKinley's casket being carried down the steps of the Capitol in Washington, D.C., in September 1901

across the nation, people stopped to remember the man who had brought prestige and prosperity to their country.

GLOSSARY

★ ★ ★

ambassador—the representative of a nation's government in another country

assassination—the murder of someone who is well known or important

campaign—an organized effort to win an election

candidate—someone running for office in an election

empire—a country that controls areas far beyond its borders

prestige—high standing

prosperity—economic well-being

puppet—a person who does, says, and thinks what someone else orders

secretary of state—the president's leading adviser in dealing with other countries

seizures—sudden attacks often associated with epilepsy that sometimes cause a person to shake violently

strike—when workers refuse to work, hoping to force their company to agree to their demands

treaty—an agreement between two governments

veteran—a person who served in the military

WILLIAM MCKINLEY'S LIFE AT A GLANCE

★ ★ ★

PERSONAL

Nickname: Idol of Ohio

Birth date: January 29, 1843

Birthplace: Niles, Ohio

Father's name: William McKinley

Mother's name: Nancy Campbell Allison McKinley

Education: Attended Allegheny College in 1860

Wife's name: Ida Saxton McKinley (1847–1907)

Married: January 25, 1871

Children: Katherine McKinley (1871–1875);
                     Ida McKinley (1873–1873)

Died: September 14, 1901, in Buffalo, New York

Buried: Canton, Ohio

PUBLIC

Occupation before presidency:	Teacher, clerk, soldier, lawyer, politician
Occupation after presidency:	None
Military service:	Brevet major for the Union army during the Civil War
Other government positions:	Stark County prosecuting attorney; representative from Ohio in the U.S. House of Representatives; governor of Ohio
Political party:	Republican
Vice presidents:	Garret A. Hobart (1897–1899); Theodore Roosevelt (1901)
Dates in office:	March 4, 1897–September 14, 1901
Presidential opponents:	William Jennings Bryan (Democrat), 1896 and 1900
Number of votes (Electoral College):	7,102,246 of 13,594,805 (271 of 447), 1896; 7,218,491 of 13,575,225 (292 of 447), 1900
Writings:	None

William McKinley's Cabinet

Secretary of state:
John Sherman (1897–1898)
William R. Day (1898)
John Hay (1898–1901)

Secretary of the treasury:
Lyman J. Gage (1897–1901)

Secretary of war:
Russell A. Alger (1897–1899)
Elihu Root (1899–1901)

Attorney general:
Joseph McKenna (1897–1898)
John W. Griggs (1898–1901)
Philander C. Knox (1901)

Postmaster general:
James A. Gary (1897–1898)
Charles Emory Smith (1898–1901)

Secretary of the navy:
John D. Long (1897–1901)

Secretary of the interior:
Cornelius N. Bliss (1897–1899)
Ethan A. Hitchcock (1899–1901)

Secretary of agriculture:
James Wilson (1897–1901)

WILLIAM MCKINLEY'S LIFE AND TIMES

★ ★ ★

MCKINLEY'S LIFE

January 29, McKinley   1843
is born in Niles, Ohio

WORLD EVENTS

1840   1840   Auguste Rodin,
famous sculptor
of *The Thinker*
(right), is born

1850   1848   *The Communist
Manifesto,* by German
writer Karl Marx, is
widely distributed

1852   American Harriet
Beecher Stowe
publishes *Uncle
Tom's Cabin*

1858   English scientist
Charles Darwin
(right)
presents
his theory
of evolution

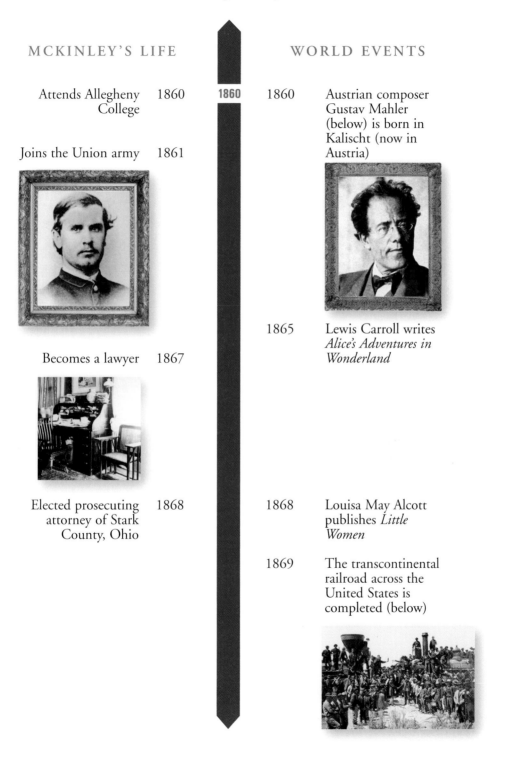

MCKINLEY'S LIFE

Attends Allegheny College — 1860

Joins the Union army — 1861

Becomes a lawyer — 1867

Elected prosecuting attorney of Stark County, Ohio — 1868

1860

WORLD EVENTS

1860   Austrian composer Gustav Mahler (below) is born in Kalischt (now in Austria)

1865   Lewis Carroll writes *Alice's Adventures in Wonderland*

1868   Louisa May Alcott publishes *Little Women*

1869   The transcontinental railroad across the United States is completed (below)

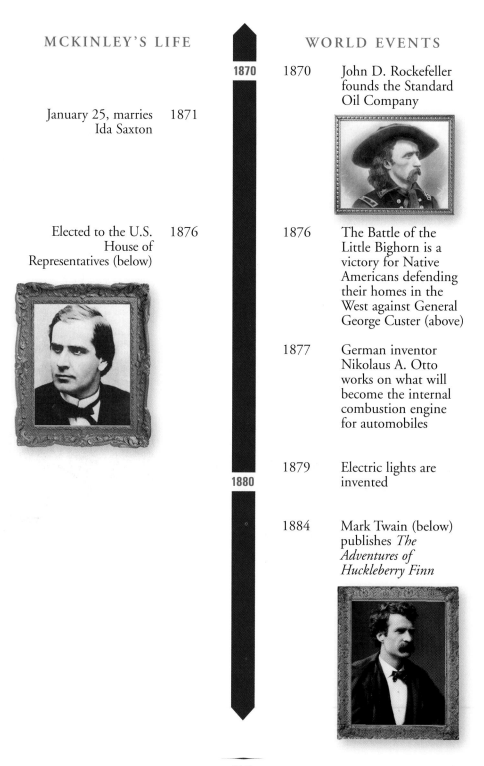

MCKINLEY'S LIFE

January 25, marries 1871
Ida Saxton

Elected to the U.S. 1876
House of
Representatives (below)

WORLD EVENTS

1870

1870 John D. Rockefeller
founds the Standard
Oil Company

1880

1876 The Battle of the
Little Bighorn is a
victory for Native
Americans defending
their homes in the
West against General
George Custer (above)

1877 German inventor
Nikolaus A. Otto
works on what will
become the internal
combustion engine
for automobiles

1879 Electric lights are
invented

1884 Mark Twain (below)
publishes *The
Adventures of
Huckleberry Finn*

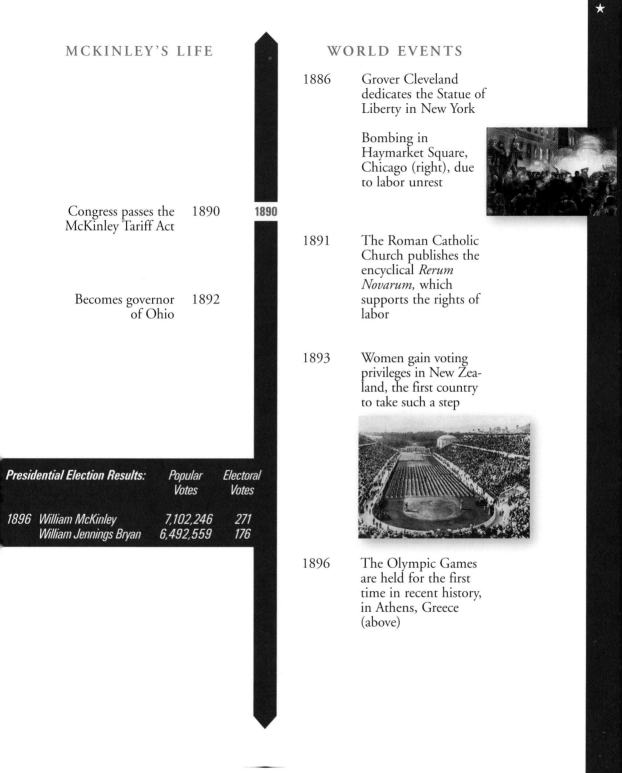

MCKINLEY'S LIFE

WORLD EVENTS

1886   Grover Cleveland dedicates the Statue of Liberty in New York

Bombing in Haymarket Square, Chicago (right), due to labor unrest

Congress passes the McKinley Tariff Act   1890   **1890**

1891   The Roman Catholic Church publishes the encyclical *Rerum Novarum*, which supports the rights of labor

Becomes governor of Ohio   1892

1893   Women gain voting privileges in New Zealand, the first country to take such a step

Presidential Election Results:	Popular Votes	Electoral Votes
1896 William McKinley	7,102,246	271
William Jennings Bryan	6,492,559	176

1896   The Olympic Games are held for the first time in recent history, in Athens, Greece (above)

MCKINLEY'S LIFE

February 15, the
USS *Maine* (below)
explodes in the
harbor at Havana,
Cuba; Americans
blame Spain

1898

The United States
defeats Spain in the
Spanish-American
War, resulting in the
United States gaining
control of Puerto Rico
and the Philippines

The United States
takes over Hawaii

People in the
Philippines rise up to
drive out U.S. forces

1899

WORLD EVENTS

1898

An avalanche on the
Chilkoot Pass in
Alaska kills eighty-
eight men searching
for gold during the
Klondike Gold Rush

1899

Isadora Duncan
(above), one of the
founders of modern
dance, makes her
debut in Chicago

MCKINLEY'S LIFE

WORLD EVENTS

Sends troops to China to put down the Boxer Rebellion — 1900

1900

Presidential Election Results:		Popular Votes	Electoral Votes
1900	William McKinley	7,218,491	292
	William Jennings Bryan	6,356,734	155

September 6, shot by an assassin in Buffalo, New York (above) — 1901

September 14, dies from his wounds

1901 — Britain's Queen Victoria dies

First exhibition of Pablo Picasso opens

The first Nobel Prize ceremony is held in Stockholm, Sweden

1903 — Brothers Orville and Wilbur Wright successfully fly a powered airplane (below)

UNDERSTANDING WILLIAM MCKINLEY AND HIS PRESIDENCY

★ ★ ★

IN THE LIBRARY

Collins, Mary. *The Spanish-American War.*
New York: Children's Press, 1998.

Joseph, Paul. *William McKinley.* Edina, Minn.: Abdo Publishers, 2002.

Poggia, Pier Paolo. *The Age of Progress and Electricity, 1850–1900.*
Philadelphia: Chelsea House, 2002.

ON THE WEB

McKinley Memorial Library and Museum
http://www.mckinley.lib.oh.us
For information about McKinley's life and presidency

The White House—William McKinley
http://www.whitehouse.gov/history/presidents/wm25.html
For a brief biography of McKinley

Library of Congress—William McKinley
http://lcweb2.loc.gov/ammem/pihtml/pi032.html
To see early Thomas Edison video footage from the
National Digital Library of McKinley's inauguration

MCKINLEY HISTORIC SITES
ACROSS THE COUNTRY

McKinley Museum and National Memorial
800 McKinley Monument Drive NW
Canton, OH 44708
330/455-7043
To visit a museum with artifacts and documents related
to McKinley's life and to see where he is buried

National First Ladies Library
331 South Market Avenue
Canton, OH 44702
330/452-0876
To see the family home of Ida Saxton McKinley,
which now houses a library containing documents
and artifacts related to the first ladies of the United States

National McKinley Birthplace Memorial
46 North Main Street
Niles, OH 44446
330/652-1704
To visit a museum filled with items
related to McKinley's life and presidency

THE U.S. PRESIDENTS
(Years in Office)

★ ★ ★

1. George Washington
(March 4, 1789-March 3, 1797)
2. John Adams
(March 4, 1797-March 3, 1801)
3. Thomas Jefferson
(March 4, 1801-March 3, 1809)
4. James Madison
(March 4, 1809-March 3, 1817)
5. James Monroe
(March 4, 1817-March 3, 1825)
6. John Quincy Adams
(March 4, 1825-March 3, 1829)
7. Andrew Jackson
(March 4, 1829-March 3, 1837)
8. Martin Van Buren
(March 4, 1837-March 3, 1841)
9. William Henry Harrison
(March 6, 1841-April 4, 1841)
10. John Tyler
(April 6, 1841-March 3, 1845)
11. James K. Polk
(March 4, 1845-March 3, 1849)
12. Zachary Taylor
(March 5, 1849-July 9, 1850)
13. Millard Fillmore
(July 10, 1850-March 3, 1853)
14. Franklin Pierce
(March 4, 1853-March 3, 1857)
15. James Buchanan
(March 4, 1857-March 3, 1861)
16. Abraham Lincoln
(March 4, 1861-April 15, 1865)
17. Andrew Johnson
(April 15, 1865-March 3, 1869)

18. Ulysses S. Grant
(March 4, 1869-March 3, 1877)
19. Rutherford B. Hayes
(March 4, 1877-March 3, 1881)
20. James Garfield
(March 4, 1881-Sept 19, 1881)
21. Chester Arthur
(Sept 20, 1881-March 3, 1885)
22. Grover Cleveland
(March 4, 1885-March 3, 1889)
23. Benjamin Harrison
(March 4, 1889-March 3, 1893)
24. Grover Cleveland
(March 4, 1893-March 3, 1897)
25. William McKinley
(March 4, 1897-
September 14, 1901)
26. Theodore Roosevelt
(September 14, 1901-
March 3, 1909)
27. William Howard Taft
(March 4, 1909-March 3, 1913)
28. Woodrow Wilson
(March 4, 1913-March 3, 1921)
29. Warren G. Harding
(March 4, 1921-August 2, 1923)
30. Calvin Coolidge
(August 3, 1923-March 3, 1929)
31. Herbert Hoover
(March 4, 1929-March 3, 1933)
32. Franklin D. Roosevelt
(March 4, 1933-April 12, 1945)

33. Harry S. Truman
(April 12, 1945-
January 20, 1953)
34. Dwight D. Eisenhower
(January 20, 1953-
January 20, 1961)
35. John F. Kennedy
(January 20, 1961-
November 22, 1963)
36. Lyndon B. Johnson
(November 22, 1963-
January 20, 1969)
37. Richard M. Nixon
(January 20, 1969-
August 9, 1974)
38. Gerald R. Ford
(August 9, 1974-
January 20, 1977)
39. James Earl Carter
(January 20, 1977-
January 20, 1981)
40. Ronald Reagan
(January 20, 1981-
January 20, 1989)
41. George H. W. Bush
(January 20, 1989-
January 20, 1993)
42. William Jefferson Clinton
(January 20, 1993-
January 20, 2001)
43. George W. Bush
(January 20, 2001-)

INDEX

★ ★ ★

ABOUT THE AUTHOR

Robin S. Doak has been writing for children for more than fourteen years. A former editor of *Weekly Reader* and *U*S*Kids* magazine, Ms.Doak has authored fun and educational materials for kids of all ages. Some of her work includes biographies of explorers such as Henry Hudson and John Smith, as well as other titles in this series. Ms. Doak is a past winner of an Educational Press Association of America Distinguished Achievement Award. She lives with her husband and three children in central Connecticut.